How to use this book

This book has two stories.

Before each story there are important activities which will help prepare your child for reading it. When he or she has read the story, there are further activities which will help reinforce what has been learnt.

☆ *Have fun talking about the pictures.*

☆ *Encourage your child to read the engaging stories again and again for fun and practice.*

☆ *Use the Star checklists on pages 3 and 13 to build your child's confidence as he or she colours in a star after each activity.*

Six steps for reading success

1 Practise reading the Speed sounds before each story.
2 Read the Green and Red words before each story.
3 Read the story.
4 Re-read the story to reinforce meaning.
5 Answer the questions about the story.
6 Practise reading the Speed words.

Give your child lots of praise and encouragement. Have fun!

Story

I can read the Speed sounds.

I can read the Green words.

I can read the Red words.

I can read the story.

I can answer the questions about the story.

I can read the Speed words.

Story The spell

Say the Speed sounds

Consonants

*Ask your child to say the sounds (not the letter names)
clearly and quickly, in and out of order. Make sure
he or she does not add 'uh' to the end of the sounds,
e.g. 'f' not 'fuh'.*

f	l ll	m	n	r	s	v	z	sh	th	ng nk

b	c k ck	d	g	h	j	p	qu	t	w wh	x	y	ch tch

Each box contains one sound.

Vowels

*Ask your child to say each vowel sound and then the word,
e.g. 'a', 'at'.*

at	hen	in	on	up	day	see	high	blow	zoo

Read the Green words

For each word ask your child to read the separate sounds, e.g. 's-l-u-g', 'm-o-th' and then blend the sounds together to make the word, e.g. 'slug', 'moth'. Sometimes one sound is represented by more than one letter, e.g. 'th', 'wh', 'ng'. These are underlined.

wi<u>tch</u>   wi<u>ll</u>   <u>wh</u>isk   <u>th</u>en

wi<u>ng</u>   mo<u>th</u>   slug

Ask your child to read the word in syllables.

cob`web → cobweb

Read the Red words

Red words don't sound like they look. Read the words out to your child. Explain that he or she will have to stop and think about how to say the red words in the story.

<u>th</u>e   y<u>ou</u>   I   s<u>ai</u>d   be   of

my   wand

Story ⭐1

The spell

Introduction

Stitch the witch likes her home to be clean and tidy. She is cross because her cat has left paw marks on her bed, so she casts a spell on the poor cat!

"You bad cat!"
said Stitch the witch.

"I will cast a spell on you!
I will whisk my wand.
Then you will be . . . a frog!"

Ask your child:
⭐ *What does Stitch the witch want her spell to do?*

7

The wing of a moth . . .
in the pot!

Six cobwebs . . .
in the pot!

The leg of a rat . . .
in the pot!

A fat slug . . .
in the pot!

"Mix it up,
mix it up . . .

abracadabra!"

Ping!

Ask your child:
⭐ *What happened in the end? How do you think the cat is feeling now?*

Speed words for Story ⟨1⟩

Ask your child to read the words across the rows, down the columns and in and out of order, clearly and quickly.

Stitch	witch	will	of	whisk
then	wing	moth	slug	I
the	in	fat	said	it
up	you	pot	cobweb	mix

Story 2

I can read the Speed sounds.

I can read the Green words.

I can read the Red words.

I can read the story.

I can answer the questions
about the story.

I can read the Speed words.

Story ⭐ 2 Black Hat Bob

Say the Speed sounds

Consonants

*Ask your child to say the sounds (not the letter names)
clearly and quickly, in and out of order. Make sure
he or she does not add 'uh' to the end of the sounds,
e.g. 'f' not 'fuh'.*

f ff	l ll	m	n	r	s	v	z	sh	th	ng nk

b	c k ck	d	g	h	j	p	qu	t	w	x	y	ch

Each box contains one sound.

Vowels

*Ask your child to say each vowel sound and then the word,
e.g. 'a', 'at'.*

at	hen	in	on	up	day	see	high	blow	zoo

Read the Green words

For each word ask your child to read the separate sounds, e.g. 'l-e-g', 'sh-i-p' and then blend the sounds together to make the word, e.g. 'leg', 'ship'. Sometimes one sound is represented by more than one letter, e.g. 'th', 'sh', 'ff'. These are underlined.

<u>sh</u>ip   peg   leg   hen   pet   box

grab   o<u>ff</u>   wi<u>ll</u>   fix   his   <u>th</u>at

is

Read the Red words

Red words don't sound like they look. Read the words out to your child. Explain that he or she will have to stop and think about how to say the red words in the story.

he   s<u>ai</u>d   no   my   I

Story ⭐2

Black Hat Bob

Introduction

Pirates are sailors who steal from other ships. Black Hat Bob is a friendly pirate, but his enemy, Red Hat Rob, wants to steal Bob's money, which he keeps in a cash box. Will he succeed?

Black Hat Bob
is on his ship.

This is his peg leg.

This is his
pet hen.

This is his
cash box.

This is Red Hat Rob.

"I will grab that cash box," he said.

"Get off my ship!"
said Black Hat Bob.

"No," said Red Hat Rob.
"I will not."

Ask your child:
⭐ *What does Black Hat Bob say?*
What sort of voice might he use?

"I will fix him,"
said Black Hat Bob.

Biff biff

Gulp!

Ask your child:
⭐ *Who do you think wins in the end?*

Speed words for Story ⭐2

ship	peg	he	said	leg
no	hen	pet	my	box
I	grab	off	get	will
fix	his	not	that	hat

Help your child to read with phonics

Sun hat fun — Book 1A

Nog in the fog — Book 1B

Get up! — Book 1C

I can hop! — Book 1D

Rag the rat — Book 2A

Nip and Chip — Book 2B

My dog Ned — Book 2C

The spell — Book 2D

Run run run! — Book 3A

Red Ned — Book 3B

Billy the Kid — Book 3C

Elvis — Book 3D

Series created by
Ruth Miskin
Based on original stories
by Gill Munton
Illustrated by
Tim Archbold

Published by
Oxford University Press
Great Clarendon Street
Oxford OX2 6DP

First published 2008
This edition 2010

ISBN 9 780192 756138

10 9 8 7 6 5 4 3 2 1

Printed in China by Imago

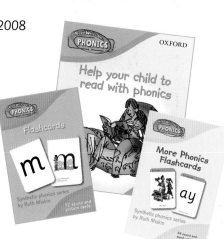